The Valley of Sorrows

L. ERICSON

outskirts
press

The Valley of Sorrows
All Rights Reserved.
Copyright © 2023 L. Ericson
v1.0

This is a work of poeticized non-fiction. The opinions expressed in this manuscript are solely the opinions of the author and do not represent the opinions or thoughts of the publisher. The author has represented and warranted full ownership and/or legal right to publish all the materials in this book.

This book may not be reproduced, transmitted, or stored in whole or in part by any means, including graphic, electronic, or mechanical without the express written consent of the publisher except in the case of brief quotations embodied in critical articles and reviews.

Outskirts Press, Inc.
http://www.outskirtspress.com

ISBN: 978-1-9772-6263-9

Cover Photo © 2023 National Archives & Records. All rights reserved - used with permission.

All photographs courtesy of the National Archives and Records Administration Department of Defense / United States Marine Corps Vietnam

Outskirts Press and the "OP" logo are trademarks belonging to Outskirts Press, Inc.

PRINTED IN THE UNITED STATES OF AMERICA

Prologue

The Que Son Valley, summer, 1967 sat, crouched like a cat, fangs bared, tail twitching, a malevolent entity that brooked your presence grudgingly. Cloaked in emerald hues of every shade,

A deception, a magic trick that fooled the eye, held and hid its secrets. An exotic place.

Beauty everywhere. A perverted beauty. A deceptive beauty. Beauty with the soul of a serial killer. Walking through it you were watched by unseen eyes. By something indefinable. Ghosts. Spirits. Specters. The hills looked down upon you, spies that ruled the Valley. Death's dark eyes, foreboding, unmerciful. It's face everywhere. Nowhere. You could… almost… see it. Look for it, it's gone.

This was an ancient place. Old when Christ walked Galilee. Old when Ganges Khan's hordes swept the steppes. You had never imagined a place this old and never wanted to see one again. Nothing you'd ever read, seen, or imagined could prepare you. Violence seemed part of it, was woven into it, and you knew, given the chance, would visit that violence upon you. You, before entering, thought you knew what scared was. You had no idea. Constantly. Fervently. Religiously.

"Forgive us our trespasses." Nowhere had those words meant more. Here the flora and fauna conspired against you. There were… Things… that crawled, slithered, bit, scratched, killed.

Snake. Scorpion, Sniper. Things without names. Things without fear of you. You may walk the Valley but you weren't the baddest thing in this Valley.

"Forgive us our trespasses."

No forgiving. No forgetting. No absolution.

The scars of war are not easily seen

In the lives we live between

Setting foot on the shore

The many lives we've lived before

And in these pages you may find

All those lives you left behind

Like no going home again

From whence your life began

So come and walk the trails and hollows

Where your lives weren't owned only borrowed

Where for everyday lived you sacrificed your tomorrows

Way out here in the Valley of Sorrows.

TICK TICK TICK

Some folks wonder what makes you tick.

(elephant grass and punji pits)

Why you're not like other folks.

(Bouncing Betty and napalm smoke)

Why you've got a bit of a temper,

(scorching sun and monsoon weather)

Why you keep it all inside.

(60 wounded and 18 died)

That what bothers them runs off your back.

(midnight mortar attack)

Why sometimes you sit and stare.

(overhead tracers and flares)

Yep, some folks wonder what makes you tick.

   tick tick tick tick.

The sun was shining on the ville

looked like Heaven smelled like Hell.

The peanuts were drying on a mat

in front of which Mama san sat.

Two water boo were giving us the eye

there's not a cloud in the sky.

The Angel of Death was sitting near

stoking the fires of fear.

And all around came the sound

of jungle boots striking the ground.

Oh, what a bloody mess

"Bang"

said the sniper in his nest.

Just another day in the Devil's domain

8000 miles

from Wilshire and Main.

He had a 60 Chevy with a 348.

Had a girl he used to date.

He had a .22 when he was 12.

Thought he knew the difference between Heaven and Hell.

Took her to the drive-in two towns over.

Bought her some candy from Russell Stover's.

Had everything a young guy could want.

Had 3 uncles and an aunt.

He used to dream about all he'd lost.

Used to say it was just the cost.

Just the cost of doing what's right.

Used to say it after every firefight.

Said it when he climbed the mountains.

Said it when mortars rained down like a fountain.

I asked him, "What are you going to do when you get back?"

This was the morning after the attack.

But not a word came from his lips.

I think he knew it was a one way trip .

There's a young guy lives inside of me
And he's only 18
Nothing wrong with his hips, back, or knees
His eyesight's good his hearing too
There's not a thing he's afraid to do
Take a corner at 90 miles an hour
Drink and smoke a bit of the wildwood flower
But he'd really like a nice hot shower
A hot shower and dry feet
A four poster bed in which to sleep
Sunday dinner would be a treat
But of all that
A hundred rounds is all he lacks
Knows just what he'll do when he gets back
Yep, he's still 18
The kids still got all his dreams
Got his dreams, wishes, and wants
Gets a kick out of haunting me
When I'm reciting the Rosary
But me and him we've made our peace
Him with his dreams and me with my knees.

With Honors

Every bone in his body hurt
from head to toe he was covered in dirt
hadn't a shower in 3 weeks
was bitten all over by a leech
had running sores on his feet
on his back an empty pack
shared a hole with his buddy Jack
23 days in the bush
every day an adrenaline rush
he'd dropped 30 pounds
fired off 300 rounds
blew 4 duds and a tunnel
used his helmet for a funnel
to look at him you'd never know
he graduated high school 8 months ago.

When it rained you got wet

When it was hot you got the sweats

When night came you dug a hole

Then the mosquito's took their toll

23 days without a bath

23 days you only napped

Ate your meals from a can

Left you looking like a skin and bones man

Off your body had your clothes rot

Then you got … shot.

A man of few words.

He spoke in a foreign tongue
always going on about the stars and sun
monsoon rains and caravan runs
how the night hid the day
and the price one paid
the cost of an early grave.
And if you listened you'd not hear a word
only the song of the birds
nothing he said could be heard
for the language he spoke was in code
when he cleared his throat
eyes wide mouth shut
whispered from the bottom of a rut
a thousand words in each glance
a thousand more in his stance
words he spoke in a chant.

Every day under the sun
he speaks in a foreign tongue
learned when he was young
a story heard by none
told in his eyes the way he walks
from a man who seldom talks .

He had lain there all night,

played dead as the NVA moved among them.

Held his breath as they searched, stripped away the gear, weapons, ammo, grenades,

finally moving off into the darkness.

Imagine, if you can, his nightmares.

There's no imagining.

Even we, who were there, cannot imagine that.

Operation Union
13 May 1967

It's 3 a.m. in the land of the dove
the moon and stars shine down from above
says to himself "I'll be a son of a whore,
did I lock the back door?"

Then room by room he creeps
into each corner he peeks
just like the days 50 years ago
inching through the paddies and hedgerows
when he packed everything on his back
now in every room he could be attacked
dares not turn on the lights
it'd be like being in a firefight
finally reaches the door
"Damn it ,locked "
like a hundred times before.

Lessons learned from a time
when he learned the whine
of AK rounds and rockets roar
checks the clock it's a quarter till four
In the land of the dove it's all out war.

Maybe you never got shot

maybe malaria is what you got.

Maybe you were never in a fire fight

maybe for you it was a rocket lighting up the night.

Maybe you never ate out of a can

maybe it was a mortar shell that made you a man.

Maybe you never flew the skies

maybe there were other ways you could die.

Maybe you never cleared the dead

maybe you lost a buddy named Fred.

Maybe you never bathed in a river

maybe it was a rat in your hootch that made you shiver.

Maybe we really fought our own war

maybe,maybe,and maybe some more.

Maybe it still knocks at your door .

Full grown men who looked like kids till you knew what we did.
Where we went , what we saw.
We weren' kids anymore.

He was a small town kid from the wrong side of the tracks

but he always had my back.

I didn't care if he grew up in a three room shack

'cause without him I wouldn't have made it back

and he says the same about me.

He use to call me Bo Diddley

and I called him Whacked

cause when you're sitting back to back

There weren't no wrong side of the tracks .

Did you ever see a Cobra fly?

Ever see a truck hit a mine?

Ever see 60 wounded and 18 die?

Ever think the sun would never rise?

Ever see a trip wire across a path?

Ever see a corpsman breathe his last ?

Ever think your time had come?

Ever stand your ground when your brain screamed run?

Ever see a man jolt

like he was hit by a lightning bolt?

Ever wish you were dead

after watching the dead hold on by a thread?

All the answers lay in our past

to all the evers never asked .

Que Son
The Valley of Sorrows

They're getting ready to put a man on the moon

while we're crossing this leech filled lagoon

through the water up to our waists

one eye looking for Charlie the other looking for snakes.

Down on the Cape the rockets roared

while we were crossing from shore to shore.

They say they'll have him there in '69

between now and then there'll be a whole lot of dying.

And they say we're the mightiest country on earth

but in the Valley all we're wondering is who'll die first.

The Valley of Sorrows
L.Ericson

There's a flag flying on a hill

over a house where time stands still.

In that house stands a man

who fought a war in Viet Nam.

In that house that man naps

dreams of bombs and booby traps

sees the faces of those men

those who stood next to him.

Every night that flag flies

every night he sees them die

in a house on a hill

in a house where time stands still .

Panel 18 E

18 when he left

18 when he died

18 cousins at his casket cried

18 words the preacher said

18 roses by his head

18 times her heart cracked

18 tears fell in her lap

18 years since he was born

18 years are not that long

18 summers come and gone

18 years she aged that day

18 years later she passed away

18 roses by her head

18 words the preacher said

18 times the bell toned

18 words on her stone.

Dear Mom

We wrote lies.

Everything's fine.

(18 guys died)

The weather's been hot.

(another guy got shot)

We're going to China Beach.

(got bit by a leech)

Can you send some hot sauce?

(a patrol went out all were lost)

Well guess that's all,see you soon.

(the op starts at noon.)

Didn't do it for the money

there was no money to be had.

Didn't do it for Jesus, Uncle Sam, or the Flag.

Didn't do it to impress my old man.

Didn't do it because I hated the enemy.

Didn't do it to keep people free.

I did it for the guys who were there with me

did it for them and they for me.

Did it so some would come home alive

did it so some would survive

did it for those who died.

I did and I didn't

and that's the truth in it.

Hell of a way to live a life

staring through that 18 year old kids eyes

twitching at a twigs snap

hitting the ground when thunder cracks.

Enemies , enemies everywhere

not even safe sitting in your old chair

catching movement just out of sight

staring out the windows in the middle of the night.

Hell of a way of reliving the past

that has never passed

just as fresh as the morning dew

seen through eyes that see through you .

Horrendous
were the wounds of war
some looked like they were made by a saw
wielded by Jack the Ripper
who opened them up like a zipper
or by Lizzie Borden and her ax
after the forty whacks.
Some would make you shake your head
Wonder how they weren't dead.

The body could take some terrible punishment
on others a wound there wasn't
Felled by a tiny bug
or by the sun above.

There was no rhyme or reason
every day a killing season.

If you escaped and not many did
the other wounds you kept hid
in a jar with a child proof lid.

It was a damn shame
that for some
their last meal came out of a can..
20 years old.

Their last letter was old news
from three weeks ago.

Their clothes were rotting away
even as their bodies were falling apart.

That they hadn't been paid
and never would.

These
things
remain
unknown
among
the masses
thus ,truth is forgotten
and history
passes.

You may have thought you'd seen it all then you saw the bombs fall.
Saw them hit , heard the boom, right on top of 3rd platoon .

Heard a guy say we were living on borrowed time

Bullshit , I said, I paid for mine.

Paid it in blood in the paddies

Climbing the hills

Carrying the bodies

Paid it in sweat

Paid it in time

Paid it with my body, paid it with my mind

Counted the days

One hour at a time

Paid it digging out the mines

Saw the price in the eyes

Of everyone that died

So , no, I never borrowed time

I paid top dollar for mine.

There's an old guy sitting on the porch

Fires up a Pall Mall with his torch

On the lighter are some words

The American flag and a sword

That old lighter has seen some wear

Like the old guy sitting there

He got it when he was in his teens

Lot of living in between

But you know every time he spins the wheel

Kind of makes life real

Just like back in the day

When he wasn't but a step away

And his eyes get a sheen

When he spins the wheel on his time machine.

Climbing mountains, crossing streams

2 on 2 off no time to dream

23 days eating out of a can

The rest of your life not giving a damn

Easy come easy go

Heaven above Hell below

Got your hands wrapped around the stock

Magazine in, magazine locked

A song runs through your head

Something about the quick and the dead

From the mountain comes a cry

"Why me ,Lord ,tell me why"

And I thought it a sin

No one cared to answer him.

Sometimes you can hear their words like it was yesterday.

They leave you speechless with nothing to say.

Anybody got a cigarette ?

Did you hear from Sheila yet ?

What the hell you got on your arm ?

C'mon ,what'd you grow up on a farm ?

Had enough of this stuff ?

Is that a...snake... on your chest ?

Get a letter from Sheila yet ?

Hey,remember that time ?

Are those B52's or mosquitoes flying ?

How many klicks left to go ?

Think it's gonna snow ?

What'd you have for a pet ?

Hear from Sheila yet ?

Unknown places

Nameless

Except in our memories.

The C.O's down,screaming in that paddy.

A small hill we climbed.

That huge black boulder we took cover behind.

A road we walked,crossed.

That river where the guy drowned.

That hooch where the Huey strafed us.

That treeline..Damn..remember that one.

The old papa san in the ville.

The time we set in and the gooks were in the perimeter.

What was that op out in the sands..Oh yeah..hot as hell.

That place on Highway 1 where the bus hit the mine..man.

All those places that were nameless

to us ,became famous.

And then, just to keep things interesting, they told you what your life expectancy, in battle, was.

When he left he said he'd be back
Someone came home but it wasn't the same old Jack.

Now he spends his days checking the doors
spends his nights wearing a path in the floors
sleeps in a chair when he needs to rest
got a 1911 laying on his chest.

And if you ask:
"How's it going?"

Well..
It ain't raining and the wind ain't blowing.
The leaches ain't feasting on my ass
and I ain't riding a 6x through Hai Van Pass.

Ain't belly down in the bush.
Ain't eight days into a twenty day push.
I ain't eatin fruit cake from a can.

And I sure as hell ain't in Viet Nam.

Who wants cake !

Out here there'd be no birthday cakes

No calling hours or no wakes.

No trumpets blare ,no drums would drum

For each and all the chosen ones.

Was it only eight months ago

When of the war we were told

Sitting in a high school class

Now we're in it up to our ass

Got a diploma for all the good it'll do

Don't need it in this zoo

Two months I'll be 19

Depending on what happens in between

But there'll be no candles on a cake

I'm just praying there'll be no wake.

She said:

"A penny for your thoughts."

but she didn't know what she'd bought

things that'd keep her up at night

napham and firefights

the faces of your friends

a war without end

some things are better not known

unless you live alone

tales never told neither drunk nor stoned

a penny won't buy much

won't buy a dying man's love

a heart that's bled dry

or the light going out of a dead man's eyes.

I have a list
Of all the things I miss.

Sitting in a hole
Me and George on a roll
Telling stories of our youth
Baseball and Baby Ruths.

He's from Michigan
I'm from Mass
He fishes for trout
I fish for bass.

Talking about the Pennant Race
The Tigers and Sox tied for first place
Just a couple of boys next door
Thrown into a war.

Don't know what the future brings
New cars and wedding rings
Just two guys in a hole
Talking about fishing poles.

He's got a favorite fork and spoon
Can't sleep a wink when there's a full moon
Loves to watch old cowboys show
Can't bend over to scratch his toes
Got no need for no doze
And to look at him you'd just never know
He's got a warrior's soul
Molded in the paddies and on the hills
When every clock stood still
Every patrol a rush
Walking through the trees and the brush
When the rain poured down and the blood
When every word was hush , hush , hush.
Looking at him you'd never know
With his gray hair and old clothing
He was ever one of the chosen
Told no tales did no boasting
No you'd never know
He's got a warrior's soul .

Meanwhile, back in the World,
no one wanted to hear the gory details.

It was a dark green sedan in a long dirt drive.

It was a husband holding his wife as she cried.

It was taps sounding out at dawn.

It was a family brought together to mourn.

It was all the words never said

Then it was … your son is dead.

It was the darkness of the ancient war.

It was all who looked but never saw.

It was us and them and everyone else.

Then it was those who killed themselves.

It was all we know and all you don't.

For every life lost a heart broke

It was each and all of these things

summoned by the doorbell's ring .

There's an old man up on SaddleBack Ridge
got a bad back, got a bad twitch
and there ain't a lot who remember him
back when he was 19 and thin.

But I remember him another way
back in '67 on the 13th of May.
He was firing his 60 till the barrel smoked.
Didn't flinch. Didn't choke.
He saved the lives of 15 men
but what killed him
he couldn't save the other 10
back when he was 19 and thin.

So here's to the old man on the ridge
you paid for the bad back , paid for the twitch
paid more than most men could
paid more than one man should
and that's how I remember him

back when he was 19 and thin.

We were too young to possess such old souls.
Looked from eyes that had seen more than eyes should.
Walked without the cane yet carried the crutch.

Old souls
In such young men.

Lay
with skeletons
thought as one
13 months under the gun
wept blood at the visions that come.

Watched the eclipse
saw the moon eat the sun
as old souls
devoured
the young.

We were the kids you thought you knew
Walked by your house on the way to school
Rode our bikes , slid our sleds
Played war with the other kids.

We were the ones who mowed the lawns
Delivered your paper at the crack of dawn
Hayed the field's harvested the corn.

Then came the nations call
We stood proud we stood tall.
Some came back some survived
But those kids had died
Returned older than their years
Wracked with memories , jitters , fears.

Those who flinch at the sounds.
Those whose heads spin around.
The ones who can't stand crowds.
Those who sit and stare
At things you think aren't there.

We were the kids you thought you knew
Victims of the Asiatic flu.

If someone told you at 18

You'd be building dreams

Walking the paddies in mud up to your knees

Tromping down a trail with no by your leave

Watching the flares swing in the breeze

As the rounds cracked by your ears

Afraid of everything you'd hear

If someone told you at 18

There'd be no forgetting all you'd seen

Would you stand and roll your eyes

Shake your head

Laugh

or

Cry .

Out here the water could kill you.

It might take 30 or 40 years

but still ..

I've got ghosts in my house
I catch them out of the corner of my eye
when they think I'm not looking
I'm always looking.

Ghosts in my house.
Hitched a ride home with me.
I don't remember all their names but they remember mine
and that's fine .

Sometimes
I hear them
and it ain't the wind , not a breeze
not a shadow
that's rustling the trees.

Ghosts in my house
of all the men
I called friend
saved me when I couldn't save myself.

There's one right there…

Don't stare .

There wouldn't be no Liberty Bell

No Iwo Jima or Pork Chop Hill

No storming the beach at Normandy

And that's just fine with me

Never saw Belleau Wood

They weren't making movies in Hollywood

Washington wasn't crossing the Delaware

No B 17's getting blown out of the air.

No,this was our war

None had seen it's like before

From the Delta to the DMZ

From the mountains to the South China Sea

From the jungles to the Valley floor

The RPG's and rockets roared

And the only thing it had in common

You, too, could end up in a coffin .

It's the sound of the other shoe hitting the floor.

It's the choppers whine and the rockets roar.

It's Bill and Bob,Stinky and Pete.

It's the click of a mine under your feet.

It's a dud or maybe it isn't.

It's praying to God to get you through it.

It's 2 a.m. ,not a cloud in the sky.

It's all the dead and you wonder why.

It's "Marine,you number 10".

It's wondering where you are and where you've been.

It's no cats ,no dogs,no cars.

It's no Hershey bars.

It's Heaven above and Hell it seems.

It's ten days till you turn 19.

When the little ones ask

"What did you do in the war Grandpa?"

Survived.

Came home alive.

Saw a lot of good men die.

So I could sit with you.

Teach you to tie your shoes

Watch you swing a bat.

Dress your dolls in hats.

All I did was worth all that.

To have this time with you.

Bait and switch was a game we played

Between the cradle and the grave

Silent screams of solemn men

Who went into the Valley came out again

Crossed the rivers climbed the hills

Clocks stopped time stood still

While we were looking for the secret spot

Rattled the windows shattered the locks

On each grave a forget me not

Bait and switch, cradle and grave

Many lost others saved

In this Valley time was not

But a lifetime on a broken clock

Blood, bone, guts ,screams

became our American dream.

Back in the World it was the Summer of Love.
Here in the Valley it was the Summer of Blood.

18 rounds in a 20 round mag

on your hip you've got 2 frags

5 blasting caps in a 10 cap box

1 extra pair of socks

2 ½ pounds of C4 in your pack

A 10 pound flak jacket on your back

13 cuts on your hands

elephant grass …you understand

1 bottle of bug juice on the steel pot

didn't really do squat

14 salt tabs you took today

when you sweat it runs in waves

285 days to go

praying God to make it so

It was just a numbers game

as 58,000 went to their graves.

Out here
where the snakes
slithered
where you were an enemy
of the people
invader
or savior
where every coin flipped
came up tails
we tipped
our hats to the tunnel rats
they who slithered too
where the dragon
came and went
out here where all was fair in love and war
the mountains still young
the maidens still chaste
and filled with hate
there would be mistakes
that got good men killed
and each and all got a thrill
out here where the snakes slithered
and lives withered
we grew.

It wasn't a walk in the park

Better not go out after dark

No streetlights telling you to go home

Mom wasn't calling on the phone

It was...the click of a handset

Sitting in a hole soaking wet

Safety comes off then on

100 hours until dawn

It was what you saw and what was seen

Your buddy whispering... "Sweet Dreams"

As you took your 2 hour nap

An hour in came the attack

And you,you had dreamed

You were walking Mary in the park

Street lights on after dark.

Overhead
flares light up the night
turn darkness to daylight

Canisters fall
sound like the mating calls of deranged cranes
Whoop Whoop Whoop.

Tracers fly past
red ones out green ones in.

Radio operators sing out,
India 6, over ?
India 6 ?
India Six!

60's going
16's jamming
Grunts yelling
Corpsman !

The smell
The smoke

We're all going to die .

And the kids wonder what to do with Dad

And that, my friends, is just damn sad.

What to do with the guy

Who once flew the skies

Walked the trails waded the rivers

Suffered malaria's shivers

Carried the bodies of his friends

Fought a war without end

Spent his nights in a hole

Spoke not a word told not a soul

What do we do now that he's old?

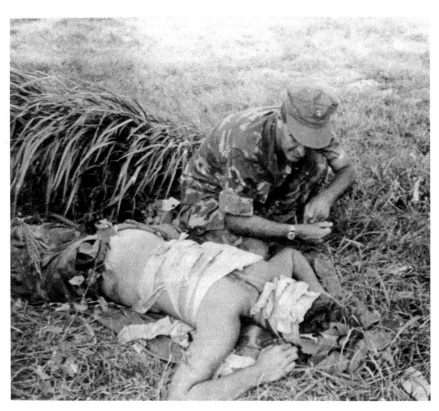

An Old Friend

Had an old friend come visit today

Brother, I said, you haven't changed

Man, you look just the same

still got the blood running from your head

still got the look of the dead

got the same jungle pants on

they're still ripped, still torn

and would you look'ee there

there's the wound that took all your hair.

What's that you say?

Yep, it's a mighty nice day.

Me?

Well, I've been fine

been toasting you with this here Boones Farm wine

got a dollar for every time I heard

he's with the Lord.

But I knew that was true.

Damn son, look at you.

One guy got killed and three guys got shot

Some might say…Well, that's not a lot…

unless you were the one who saw the light fade from his eyes

who heard another scream and another cry

were the one who tried everything you knew

to help the other pull through.

One killed and three shot

not a lot.

One killed and three shot

the price for all we've got.

One killed three shot

That…is..a…lot.

Hostile,Ground Casualty

Gun,Small arms fire

Body was recovered

A description of his death by eyewitnesses went something like this.

The first round shattered his knee

and before he started to bleed

the second hit his hand

he fell 'cause he couldn't stand

three and four tore through his thigh

five and six flew by

lucky seven came next

it went through his neck

and as eight hit his head

Well …he was already dead.

It didn't matter if you were six foot two

Or five foot four

Didn't matter what color you were

If you shot left or right

Through a scope or open sights

Didn't matter if you flew the skies

Drove a tank or a mighty mite

All that mattered to each other

The reason we call each other Brother

The thing we all knew and all could see

The one thing we all believed

I'll save you and you'll save me.

Got an old friend let's call him Paul
Came home that fall
Landed at El Toro.

13 months he'd been under the gun
13 months of monsoon rains and scorching sun
For Paul the war was done.

Went through customs his bags they searched
Then to a bus he lurched
They said don't wear your uniform
There's people out there that'd do you harm.

And so he came home
didn't telephone
At the door he met his mom.

"Oh my boy, what have they done"

It wasn't the weight that he'd lost
that gave his mother pause
it was death that stared from his eyes
death that made his mom cry
death that took her boys life
and even though he was hugging her
it was the death of the child she bore .

Old Man's Hands

I've got old man hands

How it happened I don't understand

The same that swung a detector over the roads

The same that use to lock and load

These that pulled off the leech

That buried themselves in China Beach

These that worked a P38

So I could have a bite to eat

These the ones that rigged the charge

Made small work of traps small and large

These the ones that pulled the trigger

I've got an old man's hands …go figure.

We stand upon this sacred ground

Empty spaces all around

For what is seen on this barren Knoll

As if it were a Pacific atoll

But no flag will we raise

No honored escort to their graves

Nothing here will remain

But dire death and terrible pain

Memories to be shared

Among those who were there

That send shivers yet

The day JD yelled,

"FIX BAYONETS."

There's a dreamcatcher hanging over my bed

Catches the things that escape from my head

There's me and George,Hilling too

When we were bright ,shiny,and new

There's the A4 that flew into a mountain

Dead bodies that we counted

There's a mountain peak

Where we went and couldn't sleep

If you look close you can see

The NVA who tried to kill me

I think it protects me when I doze

But only God knows

What all else it holds.

Dave told Mary

Mary told Sam

He lost his boy in Vietnam.

Didn't know what happened,probably never would,

lost somewhere in the Que Son woods.

But we remember, we were there,saw the chopper blown out of the air.

Ain't no way to tell them, no time to mourn,

Their boy began dying the day he was born.

"Could have been a doctor; that's what Dave said,

Instead of laying in a paddy ,19 years old and dead."

But what no one told him,what only we saw,

He took out a gun nest with a long black LAW.

Paid for his actions,got loaded on the bird,

"Going home to Dallas."

were his last words.

"Could have been a doctor, had the world by the ass,

now I've got to tell his mother he's not coming back."

Got a hankering to see

if the Song Ly Ly

still flows

and if they still sweep the roads.

If the waterboo still hate our ass

if they ever

paved

The Hai Van Pass.

Do the women

still spit

red

and if all those we killed

stayed dead.

If those in mass graves ,

the ones we came to save,

hold a grudge.

I'd like to know.

If truth be told.

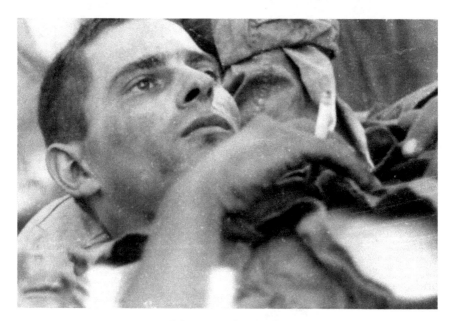

I See Dead People

This Valley we walked but left no tread

wiped up the blood

policed our dead.

If you were to look there today

there is nothing left to say

we were there then went away.

No young men to carry on the fight.

No mothers weeping at the sights.

No choppers flying at first light.

No reason to stay

not then

not today.

The only clue to our passing

are the ghosts…

and they're not laughing.

Christmas Day

St.Patrick's Day

Memorial Day

April Fool's Day

Labor Day

Thanksgiving

New Year's Day

Washington's Birthday

The Winter Solstice

Your Birthday

All these days and all the other days

But only one day mattered …

Your last day.

Out in the Valley

Me and George wait

22 days we've tempted fate

22 days eating out of a can

22 days will make you a man

Make you a man or see you dead

Got a bullet through the head

Missing an arm,missing a leg

And you said you'd never beg

But each of us know that was a lie

Just want out ,walk ,crawl ,or fly

Out in the Valley a useless plea

Out in the Valley just George and me

Flat on are bellies we both lay

Out in the Valley it's another day

Out in the Valley no two the same

Out in the Valley we've forgotten our names.

Got a bunch of guys
Went to Nam came back alive
Matt flew the skies
Duncan carried a Prick 25
Glenn was a Ranger back then
Butch was an engineer and so was Jim
I met Phil in Tam Ky
Ran into Mike and Steve Brodsky
Dave and Lenny were Sea Bee's
Joe did 2 tours
Gordon was Air Force
Moose another who joined the Corps
Wayne was on 105's
Cranking rounds saving lives
There were a couple more
Small town guys the boys next door
So here's to the Class of 65
Who went to Barre High
Each got their advanced degree
Each one a PHD .

His eyes were bugging out of his head
The first time he saw the dead
His stomach tied itself in knots
He couldn't breath,couldn't talk
He tried hard not to stare
Tried to look anywhere
But his eyes had a mind of their own
Kept glancing to that piece of ground
Saw the faces,saw the wounds
Thinking ,soon, they'll be in their tombs
In their tombs and I'll be here
Choking in the stagnant air
And that was how he got his stare.

Somewhere in the Valley live 6,000 NVA.

Something to think about on that 8 man patrol.

He came home in '67

Thought he'd died and gone to heaven

There were round eyes, round eyes, everywhere

Mustangs, GTO's, and Bel Aires

Hot showers and clean sheets

The Rolling Stones were cranking up the beat

He'd be snapping his fingers and tapping his toes

Weren't no one saying…"Man, this blows."

No c-rats, no Lp's

Not a bit of concertina could he see

No mortars going thump

Nothing he had to hump

Nothing he had to tote

Only two more years till he could vote

But sometimes he had to admit

He really missed blowing up shit.

There's an old wound that never healed
one that even time couldn't seal
it's made of sights and sounds
boobytraps and AK rounds.

Some days it itches like hell
drips blood and starts to swell
and no bandage known to man
can halt the memories that once ran
ran, then ran some more
from that festering sore

It's got a name none dare speak
neither the strong nor the weak
but those who bear the scar
those who traveled far
from the wounding place
wear it as a sign of grace
that they once stood
amongst the brotherhood
and each and all know
the scars that no one shows.

We came from the cities

came from the farms

came from the back roads came from the sticks

big city slicks and small town hicks.

We came from the mansions and broken homes

came all together and came all alone

came from the grasslands came from the South

some came single, some had a spouse.

We came from Montana's hills and Arizona's sands

came from Dubuque and the badlands

came some not old enough to shave

came when we could have stayed

came not old enough to vote

came not knowing how much ammo to tote.

We came from every realm and every where

land of the dolphin and grizzly bear

and every one who got out alive

came not knowing if they'd survive.

Didn't want to meet my Maker

be introduced to the undertaker

didn't want to lose my legs

be held together with steel pegs.

Had no desire to lose an arm

or wind up buying the farm

just wanted to come back

not strapped to a rack.

And so it came to be

came home still looking like me.

Was it fate, was it luck

was it mercy from above

or was it love?

You can run them all through your head

and never know why they died and why you lived.

Ever been to a Haunted House

with its fake witches and make believe ghosts?

Got all the ghosts that I need

and they ain't make believe.

Can still feel my hands running under his back

when I searched him for booby traps.

Can still hear another scream,scream,scream

wide awake and in my dreams.

Still smell his burning flesh

in my mind it's still fresh.

Can still feel the weight of all those I lugged

and there ain't no VA drug

to sweep that under the rug.

So,no,I never went to a haunted house

'cause I've got one myself.

Couldn't Drink   Couldn't Vote
Could Shoot a Gun

There were Dear John's and crumbled cookies

love letters and pictures of puppies

notes from the Boy Scouts

Care Packages you passed about

Tabasco sauce and grape Kool Aid

a cake that your mother made

All these back when

"You've got mail "

really meant something.

Where were all the dogs

Where were all the cats

Where were all the pools and the BBQ grills

Where were all the soda shops with the soda nicely chilled

Where were all the Chevy's,the Buicks,the Fords

Where were all the convertibles and two doors

Where were all the blondes,brunettes and redheads

Nothing here but the quick and the dead

Nothing but the rain and the blood

Nothing here but terror and dread

No Saturday night date

No getting her home late

No ass chewing from her old man

Not a damn thing here you could understand.

We, me and the squad from Mike company,

are guarding the bridge.

We sweep the road by day

guard the bridge at night.

I don't realize it but I'm working with ghosts.

Dead men who haven't yet died.

Dead men pretending to be alive.

So...to sum it up..

You've got crotch rot,jungle rot,trench foot

borderline malaria...leech bit...ant bit...

got the shits...heat exhaustion...sleep deprivation...

a bad tooth...you've lost 35 pounds...

out of water...out of butts...low on ammo...

eating a can of Ham and Mothers

while reading a Dear John letter

as someone tries to kill you

but on the bright side...

You've got a hell of a tan.

Out in the Valley the flanks were out

weren't no lolly gagging about.

No rolling the eyes, no picking the nose

no snapping of fingers, no tapping of toes.

Everyone's got their radar on

It's life and death in the Que Son.

Out in the Valley everything wants you dead

snake, sniper, and the clock in your head.

Out where every second lasts an hour

weren't no such thing as flower power

no time to stop and smell the roses

no rivers parted by Moses.

Here in the Valley on the 28th of May

tomorrow is Memorial Day

in the year of '67

the flanks are walking the paths of Heaven.

My Girl

Out in the Valley still in our teens

there's a rock and a hard place and we're stuck in between

in our hands is a weapon that should hold a girl

safeties off we go for a twirl.

Gunpowder and blood the perfume she wears

whispers of love in our ears

sings of the lives together we'll make

sings of the lives together we'll take

sleeps beside me by my right hand

She's the only one who understands.

So I take her dancing

on the Valley floor

she's my M-14

and she's a bit of

a whore.

I was looking over my DD 214

It says where I'd been but not what I'd seen

Says I went on a 13 month vacation

Says I got a medal for defending the nation

Says I was 17 when I joined

Doesn't say I looked 43 when I returned

Says when I came back I went to Lejeune

I looked it up,it was on a full moon

On one line it says I got a Purple Heart

But not one word about the battle we fought

Where it was it doesn't say

Doesn't say it was fought on Labor day

Doesn't say I was 18

10 days before I turned 19

Not a word about the 18 dead

Or a thing about the other 58 who bled

But for everything it doesn't say

I'm still proud of it to this day .

Fathers Day

Here's to all those who never got the chance

To have a father daughter dance

Never taught a son to swing a bat

Or taught their kid to catch

Here's to all the ones

Who passed on under a foreign sun.

On his helmet he'd drawn the Ace of Spades

And a calendar to mark off the days

Over his shoulder he'd slung his M14

On his hips hung 3 canteens

Around his neck his dog tags

Had a festering scar where he got hit with a frag

Both his eyes were open wide

Always looked like he was surprised

His boots were rotting off his feet

He smelled like rotten meat

He had a funny way of talking

Dragged one foot when he was walking

To look at him you'd never know

He still had 200 days left to go .

Phil's dead.

His mother got a folded flag.

A Purple Heart.

A Gold Star.

Got to say

Phil would have been 19 today.

Phil would have been 27 today.

Phil would have been ...

This is my blood which was shed for you

This is my body which was given for you

These are the stumps where my legs use to be

These are my shirts with no arms for the sleeves

These are my eyes which no longer weep

These are the ones who fought for you

These are the ones who stood for you

These are their graves as cold as could be

These are the visions that come to me

This is the debt which goes unpaid

This is the cost and this is the wage

These are the ones who would do it again

This is the beginning

And this is

The End.

CPSIA information can be obtained
at www.ICGtesting.com
Printed in the USA
BVHW050035190523
664414BV00014B/748